I AM WITH YOU

I AM WITH YOU

For Young People
And The Young At Heart
Divine words as given to
Fr John Woolley

BOOKS

Winchester, UK
Washington, USA

First published by O-Books, 2004
O-Books is an imprint of John Hunt Publishing Ltd., Laurel House,
Station Approach, Alresford, Hants, SO24 9JH, UK
office1@o-books.net
www.o-books.com

Text: copyright 1984 John Woolley

ISBN: 978-1-78099-089-7

First published in Great Britain by Crown
Reprinted 1985
Enlarged edition 1986 by Collins (Fount)
New edition 1991 by Crown (Great Britain)
Reprinted 1993
Reprinted 1993 by the 'I am with You' Foundation
New edition 1994
New edition 1996 by Arthur James Ltd
Reprinted 1997 and 1999
Reprinted 2001, 2002 and 2004 by John Hunt Publishing Ltd
This reissue first printed 2004 by O-Books, an imprint of John Hunt Publishing Ltd –
fourth reprint 2010.

A CIP catalogue record of this book is available from the British Library.
Printed and bound by CPI Group (UK) Ltd, Croydon, CR0 4YY

TO THE READER

You have probably heard of the well-loved modern devotional classic – *I Am With You* – which is helping more and more people all over the world.

While Fr John was praying, the Lord Jesus Christ put beautiful words into his mind, and told him to write them down and share them with everyone who wanted to feel His closeness, and to know His strength each day.

In this book you will find similar words from Jesus to Fr John especially meant for young people.

We know that you will learn to treasure this special edition of *I Am With You*, and use it every day.

After receiving the beautiful and divinely inspired words of this book, Fr John later chose suitable verses from the Bible in which God speaks to us directly.

This is my prayer
for you

I pray that Jesus, our Lord,
will help you and give you
strength through these
words each day.

May you, and young
readers everywhere, find
true happiness, as you
begin to discover how great
is His love for you.

May He bless you, and
keep you in His love all
through your life.

John A. Woolley.

Prayer Before Reading

Lord Jesus, as I read Your word, help me to shut out all thoughts but the thought of You.

As I receive Your word, I know that I am receiving Yourself ... to become more and more part of me.

As I receive You, I receive Your calm, Your courage, Your joy, and Your love for others.

Thank You, Lord Jesus.

My child, this universe is very puzzling for you.

I want you to know that the secret of the universe is *love*.

Before ever My love was seen when I came to the earth, it was causing worlds to be made.

Always remember that behind *everything* which you see in My universe is love. This means that God is not a far-away Creator, but caring for you all the time ... sad when you are sad, happy when you are happy.

This love will always be there for you.

Even the hairs on your head are all counted.

(Luke 12.7)

When I was on the earth, God was seen in a way in which He was never seen before. Human beings did not have to search any longer to see what God is like.

When I came to the earth it was like a *meeting-place* ... God's love meeting human beings needing help. This meeting-place is the only place where people can start *really* to know God.

Do not worry about how God has shown Himself to other places in the universe. Just be glad that when I visited the earth, people could *see everything* which they need to see of God the Father.

God loved the world so much that He gave His only Son, so that everyone believing in Him can enjoy new and lasting life.

(John 3.16)

Each day I want you to think about the Cross … the place where you are able to see, most clearly, My love.

On the Cross, I gave up all power … the only thing left was love.

Evil tried to crush love, but it could not.

My Father's victory showed the power of that love.

I want each one of My children to find the help which only I can give.

As you think about the Cross, tell Me, 'Lord Jesus, my heart is Yours.'

**For the sake of My sheep,
I surrender My life.**

(John 10.15)

3

Ask to live close to Me all through your life.

If you do this, I will start to draw you nearer to Me, and I will see you as you are going to be one day ... perfect.

As long as you go on wanting Me, I will make sure that you arrive at the place which I have planned for you – even though you often fail Me.

My child, never lose the *wish* to live very close to Me. That wish comes from Myself!

One day, you will see and know Me perfectly, and that will last till the end of time.

**It is My love
which draws you near to Me.**

(Hosea 11.4)

It is very important to think of Me as the One who *rules* over the universe. If you do not do this, you will not expect really great things from Me! Never listen to people who make you doubt that I control everything. It hurts Me when people do not see who I am.

You know that I am God the Father's beloved Son ... any other road to God will not lead you to Him. It was through *Me* that God made all which you see around you. It is *only* through Me that millions have found happiness after spending many years without any hope.

If you always think of Me as *supreme*, everything else in your life will fall into its right place.

God the Father and Myself are ONE.

(John 10.30)

5

My child, I want you to know that nothing can ever take you away from My love.

I *chose* you; that is why you can put all your trust in Me. I will save you from all kinds of dangers. Already, I have saved you from so many dangers which you have not even known about.

Only I know what is best for your future.

Remember that no matter what happens to you, I am *always* able to put things right, and help you to start again.

**No one can ever remove
My children from My hand.**

(John 10.28)

6

When you have said, or done, something which you know is wrong, you must always come to Me *straight away*.

The important thing is not *what* you did. What *is* important is that are you truly sorry about it. I want you to know that you are forgiven, straight away, when you are truly sorry, because My love for you is so great.

Remember, always, to be sorry that the wrong thing hurt *Me* ...

Even if you have said or done something wrong many times over, never believe that I do not want to forgive you. Just come, and let Me take the wrong thing away.

And remember, *always,* to forgive other people, as I have forgiven you.

I am the Lord your God ... loving, forgiving and endlessly patient.

(Exodus 34.6)

You see so many sad things around you. You see people who are ill, people who are without food, people hating each other ...

You will feel, sometimes, that perhaps God is not there, that you are alone.

I want you to say 'no' to those feelings that I am not there. I want you to talk to Me, to tell Me that you trust Me – even if things make you wonder about Me.

What people call 'good luck' and 'bad luck' do not really matter. What *really* matters is whether I share your life, whether you are living with Me, or whether you are trying to live without Me.

Tell Me often, 'Lord Jesus, I know that You are with Me, and will never let Me down'.

**Happy are those who
have not seen Me, but believe.**

(John 20.29)

8

So many of the things which you hope for do not happen. So many plans which you make go wrong. So many people can let you down.

Yes, life is full of *disappointments* – large and small – because this world is far from perfect, and because there are forces working against Me. My child, do not be defeated by disappointments. Very often I will be saving you from something – *knowing what the future holds for you.* If a thing can't be changed, accept it. If I allowed it, it won't be able to hurt you for long. Soon you will learn to be peaceful and patient when disappointments come.

Whatever may disappoint you for a time, remember that the only priceless gift is one which you have already ... Myself!

What good is it to you if you gain the whole world, but lose your own soul?

(Matthew 8.38)

It is because I lived a human life upon earth that I can *understand* those things which make you sad, those things which make life hard.

Remember that I am not only all around you, but live in you by My Spirit. This is why I feel what you feel. When life is very difficult, when you are disappointed, when you are terribly upset, My love will feel much stronger if you *share* these things with Me.

If you share life's difficult places with Me, I can always *turn them* into something which is going to be good for you.

Your sadness will be turned into joy.

(John 16.20)

10

Those who come to know Me best are those who put Me in first place!

If it is 'Jesus first', it makes all the difference to your life.

If I am in first place, if you want to please Me, you will not have to try so hard, or fail so often. You will know that you are on a journey.

If I am your Friend, you will still be able to enjoy other friends. You will enjoy those friends *even more* if I am the Friend and Master of your life.

If I am in first place, your life will be what it was *meant* to be ... the sort of life which those who try to live without Me have never found.

**Find your greatest happiness
in knowing Me.**

(Jeremiah 9.24)

Things which you can touch or see may seem more important that those which you can't ...

I came to this world to teach people that the *really* important things are invisible.

The one thing which will last for ever is My kingdom ... My kingdom of love.

Everything will fade away one day, except My kingdom.

You are being very wise if you decide now that the unseen things are important for *you*.

If you talk to Me often, if you show love and kindness to others, it means that, for you, My kingdom is more important, more *real,* than the things which the world says are important.

**My kingdom does not belong
to this world.**

(John 18.36)

My child, it will always help you to feel peaceful if you say My name, 'Jesus', often.

This can be just a whisper to yourself, wherever you are, whatever you are doing. Saying *My* Name will mean that My peace is all around you, it will keep you from danger; you will start to feel stronger.

As you become a peaceful person, you will find that others who are with you will begin to feel the same as you ... My peace will reach them *through you*.

The peace which I give you is peace which the world can't give.

(John 14.27)

13

Remember, often, how I knew about you before you were born!

Remember, each day, to thank Me that I made you, and have kept you safe. All through your life I have sent help through people who have cared for you.

Thank Me every day, as well, that on the Cross I saved you. The world would have been lost without My victory on the Cross; you are alive *now* because of that victory. Remember, always, that you *owe* everything to Me.

I want you to know how glad it makes Me when you *thank* Me, in a world where so many forget to do so.

**I have called you by your name;
you belong to Me.**

(Isaiah 43.1)

14

When I am your Friend, life is never just a matter of luck. I *control* all that can happen to you.

If you meet somebody, but wish it had been somebody else, do not worry. If you missed something which you wanted badly, do not worry. Just accept the way life works out – even the things which seem to happen by chance – as long as I am with you. All these things fit into My plan for you.

If you learn to *thank* Me for what comes to you as you follow Me, life will become so much easier for you. You will become more and more sure that I am leading you and planning for you.

All power in heaven and on earth belongs to Me.

(Matthew 28.20)

When you do not know which way to go, it can make you afraid. If you follow Me, there will be times when you will not know exactly what lies ahead of you.

If you do not know what is just around the corner, you can be sure that it is something which I see is right for you *if* you are keeping close to Me.

You do not always have to 'do something' or to 'decide something' quickly. If you keep close to Me, you will know more clearly *when* something must be done or *when* to wait patiently. You can be sure that you are just where I want you to be at that time, if you keep close to Me.

**Your Father knows
what you really need.**

(Matthew 6.8)

$\mathcal{F}$ollowing Me is all about *trust* …

You become a trusting person by asking Me to come into difficult situations, and *then* watching how I begin to help you.

If someone lets you down, if you are disappointed about something, it does not really matter as long as you have shared it with Me and are learning to trust.

Think of how a little child looks upwards with trust as it holds the hand of a father or mother. I have hold of *your* hand and you can look up at Me with trust, in the same way.

I hold you very firmly. As you trust, it means that I am *working* to meet all your needs. *Anything* which I see as right for you I can do. Tell Me *every* day that you trust Me.

I will never let you down.

(Joshua 1.5)

I want you to promise Me that you will be *on My side* through all your life, whatever may happen.

I want to be able to depend on *you* in My plan for the world. If you let Me, I will be able to do wonderful things through you; I will be able to bring light into the darkness which is there in other people's lives.

If you promise to be My servant in this world, I will always *remember* your promise. I will be using you, even at times when you have forgotten about Me for a while!

Fix your mind on God's kingdom and His justice, above everything else.

(Matthew 6.33)

Every Christian feels alone at times.

You may feel that others don't understand you, think that you are odd, or are laughing at you. When you feel alone like this, it will be easy, sometimes, to think that in following Me you have given up too much. You need not worry about this.

It is part of My making you My follower to feel at times that you only have Me!

You will find that as you learn to depend on Me, and as I begin to be seen in you, others will want what you have got.

I will always give you *much more* than you ever give up ... Those things which you have given up you will never miss.

When he found the one precious pearl, he sold everything else to go and buy it.

(Matthew 13.46)

I want you to make another promise to Me ... the most important you will ever make!

Promise Me that you will trust Me as the one hope, not just of the world, but of *your* life. Tell Me that you will always depend upon Me when other people fail you. Just remember, my child, how *faithful* I am ...

You may often forget your promise about making Me your one true hope, but I will not! I will always make sure that you come back to trusting Me after wandering away.

If I am your true hope, tell Me, often, that I am. This will give great joy to the Saviour of a world where so many forget Me.

I will look after you till the end.

(Isaiah 49.16)

$\mathcal{T}$here is a battle between good and evil forces all around you. There are real dangers for those who do not trust Me.

If you try to remember Me with you, and say My name, 'Jesus', to yourself it means that *good* forces surround you. 'Jesus' is not just a name to say; it is a power for you to use. As you say it, the kingdom of evil has to retreat.

Saying My Name does two things: First, it helps you to keep *Me* in your thoughts. Second, it means that I save you from all sorts of traps and mistakes, lifting you over dangerous places which you may not see.

My name is there to be used … use it often during each day.

I am with you to save you.

(Jeremiah 1.19)

My child, do you find that you keep making the same sort of mistakes? Do you find that you go on hurting Me by the same sort of wrong things … things which, in your heart, you don't really want to do? Do you find that certain temptations usually prove too strong? Do you feel not very brave about some things?

I want you, now, to think every day about My strength joined to yours. It does not matter how weak you may be feeling at the time. I want you to act in a *different* way now, where you used to feel weak or where you just gave up. Thinking of My strength in you, defeats will become victories. You will be surprised at what we can do together.

Remember to refuse a wrong thing *straight away* whenever you are tempted. Don't wait to *feel* strong … just *act* in a different way and you will find that I *did* strengthen you.

I will hold you up with My victorious right hand.

(Isaiah 41.10)

When I told My children that it was a narrow way, I knew the dangers lurking on each side of the road. Because My road is narrow, many people are afraid to follow Me, because they think that they will have to give up all sorts of things which they enjoy. My child, the road is narrow because I wish you to *arrive* where I want you to be.

Along the narrow way (with Me as your Friend), you can enjoy so many of life's wonderful things. You can enjoy those things *much more* because I share them with you.

The only things which can't be yours are those which will get you *lost* ... perhaps for many years ... before you come back on to the road again.

Follow Me!

(Matthew 4.19)

I have told you that I share your life ...

What does it mean to be *united* with Me? It means that, sometimes, you will feel a little of what I feel so often ... My sadness at so much cruelty in your world. You will feel a little of the loneliness and sorrow which I felt upon the earth when people hated Me, or would not listen to Me.

But listen, My child, to what is *also* yours if you are united with Me:

You can be completely victorious over all that is from evil ... either in you, or around about you.

You can let *Me* help others through you.

You will grow more and more like Me.

You will begin to do things which you could not do on your own ... and these things will *last*.

24

United with Me – like the branch united
with the tree – nothing need make you
afraid.

**I am like the vine tree;
you are the branches.**

(John 15.5)

When you feel that everything has been spoiled ... When you feel that something can never be put right ... When you lose a loved one, or a friend ...

When you feel that you cannot face the days ahead ... please remember what I have told you: Everything that happens on earth will not last.

Try to see the things which happen as *less real* than Me or My Kingdom, even though they hurt you very much. When bad things happen, think of Me *at the same time*. Remember that these things will not always go on hurting you.

This will help you to pick yourself up and to be braver than you thought you were.

**Following Me,
you won't walk in the dark.**

(John 8.12)

Do you want to do great things for Me?

First of all make sure that I really am *part* of your life ... talking with Me, reading My word, trying to be the kind of person I want you to be.

You will then find that I will *send* people to you ... young and old. You will not always know what they need, but they will be people who will be helped by a kind word, a kind act from you.

Be absolutely certain that if you are living close to Me, I pass through you to others; many, many people will find, through you, the help which they could not find in any other way.

**Without Me,
you can't do anything.**

(John 15.5)

If you know that something is wrong, do not feel that you can do it 'just this once'.

Never believe that you can go on doing wrong things on *some* occasions and refusing to do them at *other* times.

If you go on in this way, there will come a time when you can't help yourself. You will be like a castle whose walls have huge holes in them. Temptations will have become too strong for you.

My child, use My strength to refuse what you know is wrong *every* time. This will become something you can do more and more easily.

**Do what I have told you,
and you will live in My love.**

(John 15.10)

Remember that when you ask Me for something, or turn to Me for help when things are difficult, you are *giving* something to Me.

You may only be thinking about what *you* need, not about giving to Me, but that does not matter. My love for you means that I find great joy in being there for you. Yes, *every* time that you come to Me, whatever for, I am receiving something from you.

More and more *you* will find joy in giving to those who turn to you for help.

Come to Me!

(Matthew 11.28)

When something happens which upsets or worries you, always spend a few moments to talk to Me about it *straight away*. Do this, even if you feel that you must hurry to say or to do something about what has happened!

As you share what has happened with Me, I will be able to show you more clearly why it happened; there will be something important to teach you.

The other important thing is that *I am able to stop anything getting worse*.

Sharing with Me means that you will be braver – even if a situation does not change straight away. You will so often find that without your doing anything, I am at work, putting things right.

**I will be with you when trouble
comes – to rescue you.**

(Psalm 91.5)

I told you that I came to your world so that everyone could see what God the Father is like … to see His love, His power, His goodness, His beauty.

My child, I want you to have a picture in your mind of Me! I want you to turn to it often during each day. The secret of being My follower *is to practise looking away from yourself to Me*. Picture Me reaching out to you.

If you keep looking at *yourself,* you will so often feel weak, unable to do things. If you look to *Me*, it will remind you that we are *together* … that I strengthen you.

See My presence as a *light* … a light of love, surrounding you all the time. The more you look in *My* direction, the safer and stronger you will be.

Look to Me, and I will save you.

(Isaiah 45.22)

When I told My followers to say a prayer for those who hurt them, those who treated them badly, it was because I knew that prayer has great power.

Never try to 'pay back' people – even if you feel they were to blame. Pray for the person who hurt you! Sometimes you will be very surprised, next time you meet that person, how much he or she has changed. Even if a person is still not friendly, it does not matter; you have won a victory.

It is always easier for a broken friendship to be mended if you let Me strengthen you and not try to have revenge – even *saying* bad things about a person is revenge. It is only when hurtful things are said or done by *both* persons that a friendship might be broken for ever.

**If you forgive others,
you will be forgiven.**

(Matthew 6.14)

Do you feel that prayer is only 'remembering' someone, and that only what you *do* for a person is really helping them?

My child, remember that because I share your life, your prayers have *power* ... Help is being received by someone for whom you pray, even before you can do anything for them or visit them.

Yes, I will always use your kind acts. I will *also* use your prayers in a very powerful way as you learn to tell Me about your own and other people's needs.

Whatever you ask for when praying, believe that I am giving it to you.

(Mark 11.24)

Thinking about My love for you, I want you to make sure that you have that very strong *wish* to please Me.

Make sure that that wish is there all the time. You will find that whenever you choose to do the right thing, My strength to do it is there *at the same time*.

When saying your prayers each day just say 'Lord, may what *You* want be done in my life today'. All sorts of *right* things will then happen, the *right* people will meet you. You may not notice it at first, but as you want the things that I want, you and I will become much closer; you will be a more and more *victorious* person.

Happy are those who are hungry and thirsty for goodness.

(Matthew 5.6)

34

You can learn a lesson from looking at a rose.

Just think of that flower ...
  how beautiful it is;
  how lovely is its colour;
  how sweet is its scent;
  how soft it is to touch.

People enjoy a rose because of *what it is*.

It is the same with human beings. What a person *is* makes such a difference – not just what he or she says, or tries to do.

If I live in your heart, you can be sure that you will become more and more like Me and *this* will help other people in wonderful ways.

**Let your light shine for people
all around you.**

(Matthew 5.16)

35

So many of My children have found help by using Me as a *fortress*.

In a storm, people look for a place to shelter, a place where they will be safe.

Because people can behave badly, and because so many things can go wrong, life can sometimes be like a storm. You look for somewhere to hide.

My child, you have such a place ... Me.

Learn to use *My secret place* ... the place of My love. When you are unhappy, when things go terribly wrong (either through your fault, or through someone else's) just *be with Me* ... in My secret place. Think of My arms of love around you. Soon you will feel stronger, and be able to thank Me that whatever upset you can not do so any more.

I am with you ... always!

(Matthew 28.20)

You will often be tempted to give up following Me. You will feel that it is no use trusting Me. You will feel that you are missing things which others enjoy. My child, this is where so many people have taken a road which leads to nowhere; they have given up trusting Me. Just when they were ready to become really strong and victorious persons, they lost the one Friend who could really help them.

There is a force of evil which *wants* you to turn away from Me; do not listen to it. I am already doing things for you ... let Me do more!

Tell Me, more strongly than ever before: 'Lord Jesus my whole trust is in You.'

I must always come first among the things you love.

(Exodus 20.4)

My child, what did I do for you on the Cross?

First, you know that I won for you the right to be forgiven .... for wrong things to be swept away for ever.

What I also won for you was ... *freedom.* Human beings need special help to be free from things, when they can't help themselves.

By My victory over the powers of evil, I won for you a *real* freedom. You can be free from evil's influence; you can be free from the things where evil wants to keep you a prisoner ... wrong habits, temptations, dark thoughts, feelings of weakness.

All that you have to do is to *believe* in My victory and use it; thank Me every day that I have set you free to be a new and better person.

If I set you free, you really are free.

(John 8.36)

Ask Me to show you each day which are the *important* choices which you have to make. Sometimes, what you choose can change the rest of your life ... even 'little' choices. I know *which* are the really important moments of choosing for you.

You must ask Me to make you know, deep inside, when a choice is important for your future, or for someone else's future.

You can then choose, carefully and wisely, as you share the time of choosing with Me.

The Holy Spirit will show you what is true.

(John 16.13)

$\mathbf{M}$y child, whatever sort of person you are, whatever your life has been like up till now, however unfair you may think some things have been, please *remember*: I can do wonderful things for people – no matter what they are like, no matter if they feel they have not been given a proper chance

My child, I want you to prove, more and more, just how great I am.

Is anything too hard for Me?

(Genesis 18.14)

The powers of evil want you to see people around you in a wrong way. They want you to be suspicious of others; they want you to notice only the bad things in people; they want you to look down on others, even hate them.

My child, ask Me *now* to help you to see other people *as I see them.* Only I know what has made people the way they are. Let Me help you to see a person with My eye of love so that you can pray for that person, be kind and patient with that person.

If more people had trusted Me and not been blinded by evil, wars and cruelty would not have spoiled your world.

Happy are those who have pure hearts.

(Matthew 5.8)

Life can be very complicated, and sometimes you feel helpless to do anything about what you have done, or others have done.

I want you to remember *always* that nothing can defeat Me! Because all things are in My hands. I can work in the circumstances and *make* them less complicated, if you bring them to Me, and *if* you want Me to make things better *in My way*.

Even if a problem seems huge to you, I see it as simple ... because I know the past, present and future, and exactly what must be done for you.

With God, everything is possible.

(Mark 10.27)

Every day has spaces where you can spend time with Me. Or you can *make* those spaces.

The wisest thing you can do in any day is to spend time with Me. In the quietness of My presence, something of *Me* is passing to *you*!

As you spend time with Me ...
you are able to thank Me for so many things;
you are able to pray about family or others –
especially those who need help badly;
you are able to see solutions to some of your problems.

Even a minute or two reading your Bible, thinking of the things I am telling you here, is time spent in the best possible way. After time spent with Me, you always go back to the things you have to do, feeling more calm, more strong, and seeing things more clearly.

Only one thing is really important.

(Luke 10.24)

Every night, let Me have all your worries, all your plans. Let Me have everything which is on your mind, so that I can be in control.

You know that I guard you at every moment – thank Me for this, as you prepare to sleep.

I am there to *carry* things for you, so that you can just go to sleep peacefully. Those things in tomorrow, or the days afterwards, which are on your mind, (exciting things or worrying things) … just let them all come to Me. Hand them over to Me, like handing over a heavy load.

Remember that I made you! Just let yourself go into My hands, (surrendering to Me), so that My peace can be around you through the night.

Do not let your heart be troubled or afraid.

(John 14.27)

Learn to pray about *everything* ...

Many people forget that I am interested in every part of their daily life ...

the people they meet;
the jobs they have to do;
the things they read;
even the thoughts they think!

So remember that I am *very* interested in absolutely everything which happens to *you* ... Just pray about all that goes wrong, all that is difficult. You may only have a few moments to pray about something, but make sure that you do.

Whenever you pray about something, it means that I am working for you straight away.

Don't worry about tomorrow.

(Matthew 6.34)

$\mathcal{T}$here are many reasons why people want to follow Me, want to have Me as their Friend ...

All the time, thousands are giving their lives to Me.

When a person feels he or she needs Me, it is because I had *already chosen* that person. My child, I chose you to share life with Me because I saw what you could become if I was your Friend *for ever.*

In your prayers each day, always *thank* Me that I chose you.

Yes, there are many things which I need to change in you, but because I chose you, you will always be precious to Me.

You did not choose Me; I chose you!

(John 15.16)

I have told you that My love is a *power* … one which made the universe.

I want you to think much about My love, and see it as a powerful *influence* upon you, now.

Thank Me that the influence is making you strong, making you peaceful, making you hopeful, removing all sorts of dangers around you, supplying you with all you need. Thank Me for all that My influence is doing.

My love's influence reaches from heaven to right where you are, and *makes a difference* to your life.

Just go on living in My love.

(John 15.9)

There will be times when you feel that no one *really* cares about you. You will be like those, throughout the world, who have that feeling *all the time.*

One of the things which I do for My children is to make up for any human love which is not there.

This is why so many of My children with no one to love them have found God's love – rather like finding the one precious pearl.

My love is not just one more thing to add to human love. It can be *all* that a lonely or unloved person needs.

**I Myself am all the wealth
you really need.**

(Numbers 18.20)

My child, train yourself to think about the future being *in My hands*. Train yourself to think about the time when all the sad things which happen on the earth will disappear or be made right again … the time when My Kingdom will be victorious.

When life is very hard, learn to *bring the future into the present*. Say 'Lord Jesus, thank You that this is not going to last'.

It does not matter if you can't see *how* things are going to get better. What matters is that they *will* get better, because your life is in My hands. Learn to let the light which is there in the future shine into the present, when there are struggles or sadness.

**To be with Me,
and to see My glory.**

(John 17.24)

All the time, even if you do not notice it, something is coming from Myself to you.

What happens when you trust Me is that you enjoy My *supply*. I bring what you need, at the time when I see that you need it.

Try to imagine Me with My arms outstretched towards you ... never failing to bring you what you *really* need. Think of this *supply* every day.

Thank Me for the strength, the protection, the hundreds of things which I send ... even without you asking, even before you realise that you need them.

**Before My children call out to Me,
I will answer them.**

(Isaiah 65.24)

Happiness is what most people are looking for, but if you look for happiness in the wrong places, it will only last for a very little while.

I have told My children that *My* joy must be in them. As you walk along the road which I show you, as you become more and more sure of My love, you will know a feeling of peace and of hope, which is part of true happiness. This happiness does not depend on what happens to you from day to day.

True joy is quiet but *steady;* you will find that it is yours when others, who look for happiness outside Me, have lost it.

No one will ever take your joy from you.

(John 16.22)

My child, did you know that, as I share your life, there is an *influence* going from you to others?

Even more than the kind things you say or do, it is this influence which makes a difference for the people you meet.

If you are keeping close to Me, remember that I am in *every* meeting, *every* friendship. I know exactly *how* I can use you as My servant. Always tell Me that you want to be used in *My* way.

So many people will be helped by you, if you simply let Me work, if My influence can *flow* through you.

If I live in you, and you live in Me, you will produce much fruit.

(John 15.5)

When I gave My life for the world, it was so that God and human beings could be brought together again.

When people who were enemies become friends, it always brings great joy to Me.

My child, have you found, already, how happy it makes you when you make friends after a quarrel? This is because, when a quarrel is forgotten, you are experiencing My Kingdom of love in a special way.

Even when you feel that someone else is to blame, let it be *you* who tries to bring you together again.

You are then helping to mend a place which had become damaged in My kingdom of love.

**Be good friends;
be peaceful with each other.**

(Mark 9.50)

Unlike even the best human beings, I never change.

If you have asked Me to be the Friend of your life, I will make plans for you which *must* happen, as long as you go on living with Me.

Many people turn away from Me because they do not see their prayers answered straight away. You must always be sure that *your* prayers are being answered in the best possible way. Thank Me every day for this, and thank Me every day, that I am *faithful*.

.... giving good things to those who ask.

(Matthew 7.11)

Those who love you most will try not to let you down, but remember that no one is in control of all things, as I am.

This is why you must always rely completely on Me in *every* part of your life. This is known as *banking upon Me*. If you bank upon Me, you will know deep inside you that I can not fail you.

My child, you would never be mean with someone you loved very much. So do expect the very best of Me because of My love for you. There is nothing which needs to be changed that I cannot change. As you bank on Me, you will see more and more of your prayers answered.

I am a faithful God.

(Deuteronomy 7.9)

You will often want to pray for someone who seems to need My help badly.

Sometimes you may ask Me to make them well again when they are ill, or to cheer them up when they are sad, or to send them help when they are poor or hungry.

Remember that only I know what a person really needs. Something which you can always ask Me to do is this: *Ask Me to help a person to know My love for them.*

I have all sorts of ways of doing this, and because I *want* more and more of My children to know My love, I will always answer that prayer.

Ask ... and it will be given to you.

(Matthew 7.7)

Never believe that you and I are totally different. Never believe that you can't grow to be like Me.

Remember that human beings were made to be like God the Father. This means that when you give your life to Me, everything which you see in Me ... can be yours, too. You start to be more like Me ... more of Myself in you.

It would be a much better world if My children who believe in Me *used* those things which they see when they look at Me, and which can become theirs more and more.

God made human beings in His own likeness.

(Genesis 1.26)

When you try to help someone, it does not matter how weak you feel.

What really matters is that you just allow yourself to be *with* someone and to let My love reach that person.

Through history, My servants have found how people have been helped through them, *even when they felt that they could not give anything.* They were just there ... and I did the rest!

**My strength can best be seen
in your weakness.**

(2 Corinthians 12.9)

$\mathcal{T}$he way to become a really victorious person is to choose a definite thing which you would like to conquer ...

This can be a bad habit, part of you where you feel weak and can't always make a proper effort, somewhere where you keep failing ... Ask yourself very quietly 'Do I believe that God can make me strong here?'

If you believe that I can, then decide to conquer a new thing every day. I will *always* strengthen you. Whatever victory you win, go on being victorious in that thing day after day.

**Because I made you,
I am able to carry you.**

(Isaiah 46.4)

I want you to learn to *turn away* from what is false or dangerous, things which would take you off My road.

You know, already, that things are not always what they seem; you can be led away by them, until you realise that you have been foolish.

Learn to look *straight ahead* to Me, as I lead you along My road. keep your eyes on the light, and do not wander into the dark places.

When I said that I was the Light of the World, it was to show you that you need never walk without someone to guide you.

If you keep looking towards Me, then you will *finish* the journey which leads to heaven.

**The way leading to destruction
is a broad one.**

(Matthew 7.14)

Because you can be so busy at times, you can forget the things which are important for you.

My child, remember that even when *you* forget the things which are important for you, they are in *My* mind ... I will make sure that what is right for you will happen, even if you are sometimes forgetful or unwise.

**A mother may forget her child,
but I do not forget you.**

(Isaiah 49.15)

When you pray for yourself, or for someone else, make sure that you are *believing* right!

Believe in My love.
Believe in My *wish* to help My children.
Believe in My power.

At the start of every prayer thank Me for My love and for My power. It will then become the sort of prayer which you will see *answered* more and more.

The more you pray, the more you will find Me showing you *what* to pray for and *who* to pray for. I will put these things into your mind, and because I have done so, you can be sure that I am going to give you what you ask for.

If you believe, *anything* is possible.

(Mark 9.23)

62

$\mathcal{A}$sk Me to show you what is *true*.

You must be able to see the things which are pleasing to Me in the world, and those which are false or which mean danger.

If you really want to see things with *My* wisdom, you will find yourself making fewer and fewer mistakes; you will fall into fewer and fewer things which hurt Me.

My child let Me put into you more and more of My wisdom.

I am the Truth.

(John 14.2)

You will often be very disappointed ... with yourself! You will feel that you have let Me down *too often*. You may even feel, sometimes, that I have given you up.

My child I want you to *know* ...
 that I will always be your Friend;
 that I still need you; that I forgive you;
 that I will always walk with you through this world.

Always let Me help you to *believe in yourself* again ... as I believe in you.

I will forget about your sins.

(Isaiah 43.25)

My child, always be very careful what you *think* ...

Evil will try to lie to you; it will try to make you have thoughts of anger, of jealousy, of being better than others; it will try to make you wish for revenge.

All thoughts like these are part of the kingdom of darkness. When you find yourself thinking in these ways realise straight away 'These thoughts do not come from Jesus'. Then, turn to Me and *stop* those thoughts. I will help you do so.

If you *go on* with a dark thought, it can lead to words or actions which may never be put right; these would become like a shadow over your life with Me.

**It is impossible for a good tree
to produce bad fruit.**

(Matthew 7.18)

It is not how fast you travel, but the direction in which you are going which is so important.

So many of My children have travelled very slowly, with lots of falls on the way, and you may feel that this is like you! Do not worry about this, as long as you are going in the right direction. In the end you will arrive – as long as you keep trusting Me.

Because I made you, I know the things which can slow you down, but I will always pick you up again if you *want* to continue along My road.

Whoever keeps going until the end will be saved.

(Matthew 24.13)

Try to see what lies behind the way in which people behave. If someone is unkind or unfair, remember that the power of evil *prods* people into these things.

So many do not see how very *active* evil is in causing quarrels and hatred.

Try to learn to see evil as the real enemy, *not* the person, whenever you possibly can, so that you can pray for that person.

**Pray for those people who
treat you badly.**

(Matthew 5.44)

My child remember that the strength you need for *anything* is already in you.

Use that strength, both in the big challenges, and in the hundreds of difficult choices each day.

Start to use that strength *automatically* – without needing to ask Me for it.

... given power from heaven.

(Luke 24.39)

I have told My children that they must have their treasure in heaven.

Your heavenly treasure will grow by ...
    every kind thing you do;
    every prayer you say;
    every time you refuse something wrong;
    every time you tell someone about Me.

No kind or good thing which you do on earth is ever wasted. You will be able to enjoy that treasure, *because of the sort of person you have become* on the journey through life.

**Well done,
good and faithful servant.**

(Matthew 25.21)

Do you feel afraid of some of the things which lie ahead of you?

Do you feel that you won't have the strength to meet those things?

Just remember that I go before you.

I am ready in those places when you reach them; however frightening they may seem now, you will be surprised how I will help you through them.

When you think about something in the future and feel doubt and fear, just remember the Friend who has gone ahead of you and thank Me that I *will* be there to help you.

**I go ahead of you; I will be with you,
so do not be afraid.**

(Deuteronomy 31.8)

As you find what a difference I make to your life, as you find how patient I am in all your failures, how I go on loving you, how I do things for you which no one else can do, you may find yourself using the word 'wonderful' about what I am, and what I do for you.

This is what is known as *true praise* ... something which is not made up, but comes from a child who just feels *grateful*.

I am the Bread of Life.

(John 6.35)

It is important that you learn early in your life how to use My strength when tempted to think, say, or do things which are wrong.

Following Me, you will find yourself hating mean and unkind things more and more. You will *want* not to do them.

Have that picture in your mind of Me surrounding you and helping you.

If you *use* My strength, the temptations will grow less strong.

Do not be like the people who have thought, said, and done wrong things for so long that they can't help themselves any more.

Be alert and pray, so that you won't give way to temptation.

(Matthew 26.41)

72

Learn to see Me in what is around you.

This will be not only in the beauty of My world, the things put there for you to enjoy.

I will be seen in the things which not everyone can see ...

see Me in people who are brave when suffering pain or poverty;
see Me in people who are very kind to those they hardly know;
see Me in the person who says a very wise word when you are puzzled;
see Me at work when someone changes from anger to being friendly.

My child, just notice Me in this world whenever light begins to shine where there was darkness.

**When you really look for Me,
you will find Me.**

(Jeremiah 29.13)

Many things hurt Me, but what hurts Me most is when someone stops loving, stops caring about what happens to those around them.

Even if you fall into all kinds of temptations, even if people are disappointed with you, and blame you about these things, remember that you must not lose hope as long as you never stop loving others, as I love you.

Love one another.

(John 15.12)

My child, when you wake, thank Me for bringing you safely into a new day. Then ask Me to *take you* through that day, and all that it contains. Ask Me to *take you into* what you know about, or what is unexpected. Bring every detail to me.

This will mean that you will never be alone in any part of that day. And *never* without My strength!

**I am with you,
to prosper all that you do.**

(Exodus 33.14)

I look to see if My children want to please Me, if they are ready to give up something to please Me.

When I see that you really are trying to please Me, even when it is difficult, it is not long before you find the *other* side of what I want from you ...

You please Me not only by your obedience; you also please Me when you *enjoy* My gifts in your world, when you feel peaceful, when you feel My love every day.

The child who *obeys* when it is hard, finds that in My love, I *give* so much ... to make life *easier*

Your will be done.

(Matthew 6.10)

People do not always understand you, or even try to do so.

It can make you unhappy when you have tried hard, but people do not really know, or seem to care, how you feel. The world just seems to pass you by without noticing – even your loved ones may do this at times.

My child, just remember that there is One who understands you perfectly. You do not have to explain anything to Me.

Even when you have behaved badly and are sorry, you just come to the One who *understands*. It is not just the understanding of God who is wise but God who loves ... To know that you are understood – *really* understood – will help you in so many difficult places in the future.

**As your Creator,
I will never forget to help you.**

(Isaiah 44.21)

77

The truly happy people always have *thankful* hearts.

You can always find things for which you can thank Me. Even when life is very hard, there is still a 'thank you' to be said.

Thank Me for the gift of *Myself*: thank Me for the better times which *must* come for you. If you thank Me not only for blessings now, but in the future, you will be stepping into that place where *all* My promises will have come true.

I am the Good Shepherd.

(John 10.14)

You must not let your *moods* depend on what is pleasant or difficult for you at a particular time.

What I want for you is to be a steady, calm and hopeful person *whatever is happening*. It will not always be easy, but the strength, calm, and hope will come from *Me*.

If you share everything with Me, you will find, more and more, that how you feel deep inside will *not* depend on the circumstances of each day.

Make sure that your wealth is in heaven.

(Matthew 6.20)

There is much which can make you afraid in this life. It is natural to be afraid of losing a loved one, of becoming ill – of so many things.

I want you to look *beyond* the things which can happen to you in this life. I want you to tell Me 'Lord Jesus, because You are caring for me, I have nothing to fear'.

In your world there *will* be times of darkness but it will help you not to fear if you remember that your Friend will *always* be there with you.

Therefore, let nothing make you afraid. Your only real fear must be that of living a life which brings hurt to Me.

**Little flock,
you must not be afraid.**

(Mark 4.40)

Do you *see* why it is so important to keep close to Me, and to try to live in the way which I have shown you?

If you do, I am seen in you ... I am *reflected*, and this will help so many others to come to Me, as you have done.

I in you.

(John 15.4)

As you think much about My love for you, every day, you will be more and more ...

peaceful ...
courageous ...
hopeful ...
wise ...
patient ...
filled with love for others ...

Just think of how many things come from letting your thoughts be upon My love!

Make sure that My love is not just a thought, but that it makes a difference to each day.

My love for you is an *everlasting* love.

(Jeremiah 31.3)

Yes, my child, I am *always* close to you. But try to be where you can *feel* that closeness ...

Especially remembering those times *alone with Me* to pray ...

Come and meet with Me.

(Psalm 27.8)

I invited My children to leave their burdens for Me. People can feel that they are carrying a heavy load all through their lives.

I am ready to lift *all* your burdens of worry and sadness, so that you can go through life with a sense of lightness ...

Never carry burdens which you don't need to carry – including burdens about the days ahead of you.

I will give you rest for your soul.

(Matthew 11.28)

When you receive My word, it is not only guiding you and teaching you. There is an *influence* from My word, because *I am in it.*

You will not only be wiser because of My word, but be stronger to do what I say because of that influence.

Although creation will come to an end, My word will last for ever.

(Matthew 24.33)

My child, when you know that a thing is true and right, always follow it if you can. Do not invent reasons for not doing so.

And never *pretend* to yourself that a thing may not be true, or may not be important to do, just because you don't feel like doing what is right at that time. The more you do not follow what you know in your heart is true and right, the more lost you will become.

**My sheep hear My voice,
and they follow Me.**

(John 10.27)

Do not try to get for yourself all the things which the world says are important. It is good for you to work hard, and to be rewarded and for people to say 'well done'. But never *try* to be very popular, or famous, in the eyes of the world. These things will not last.

Being loved by Me, being used by Me ... these things will last for ever. If you practise thinking about this, nothing in the world will be able to make you wander from My road!

The last shall be first ... and the first, last.

(Luke 13.30)

Begin to see the many ways in which My love affects your life. My love plans a very narrow but safe road for you, in the same way that you would steer through to safety a little child given into your care in a busy street.

Because you are always in My thoughts, and because I am your *Friend,* I wish to bring you, safely, through every difficult place. This word to you, now, is My love patiently teaching you! The wisdom which I give to you comes from that same unchanging love.

Just take for granted My *constant* protection; My *constant* good influence upon you.

In My love, live a life of *giving* and *receiving.* Including, of course, giving to *Me* and receiving *from Me.*

When you feel afraid, make it a habit to think of My love – seeing Me all around you, and holding you up.

The fear will always grow weaker when you do this, or disappear completely!

**Do not be afraid;
I go with you all the time.**

(Isaiah 41.10)

People so often doubt what I am able to do, but that is only because they have never trusted Me and *proved* what I can do. I want you to prove how powerless are the forces of evil when you really trust Me.

Where else can you go to find your deepest needs and wishes met? Call upon My help *more*. Discover how you are able to meet life's difficult places in a new way ... discover how you can *live above yourself.*

If you do *your* part when choosing, you will find that I always *complete* the victory.

Whenever you give any problem to Me, just leave it with Me, and do not try to work it all out, anxiously, yourself. How calm you can be whenever you allow Me to work! When you find that you have made progress, never surrender those gains; trust Me to help you to hold on to them!

I will care for you to the end.

(Isaiah 46.4)

90

Think every day of the deep understanding which lies within God, since the time that I stepped into history and shared your human life. What it means is that you need *never hesitate* to come to Me; My understanding will swallow up that sense of failure, those feelings of disgust with yourself, your feelings of uncertainty. I will never allow more than you can bear, strengthened by Me.

My understanding covers all the decisions you have to make, the problems you meet, your possibilities, the things which may worry you. If you let Me, I will use *every* difficult thing to make your trust stronger, and to teach you.

I only permit difficult things to *remain* in your life for as long as they serve My purposes for you! Look at My promises in the Bible, and in My word to you here, and realise that they are not too good to be true!

I will never forget you.

(Isaiah 49.16)

My child, you must understand the *holiness* of God. In My kingdom, I do not permit the things which darken your world.

You see in Me a *pattern* for you to copy ...

Yes, I know that you feel so far away from becoming like Me, but, using My strength, you can move towards *true* holiness; My holiness is not a thing to fear, but is made up of such things as gentleness, love for others, truth, peace, courage, joy ... things which will become part of you as you live with Me, and begin to see the world as I do.

Everything that I have commanded you is within your grasp. Living within you, I make you *want* to choose what is good and wise; I help you to show kindness (even when you may not feel like doing so). This is the path of true happiness. The more you obey, the clearer things become. I *want* you to feel sure of Me all the time and to show you when you are allowing something which will make Me less real.

Crowd out dark thoughts by thinking of My love, and about the things which your loved ones and friends may need.

You must be perfect!

(Matthew 5.48)

I know that you want to please Me by being kind to those around you. Just make sure there is nothing in the way you live which *stops* My using you as I really want to.

Make sure that wrong ways are conquered.

If not, you are like a pipe through which only a trickle of water can flow.

By holy ... as I am.

(1 Peter 1.16)

My child, it will help you when times are difficult, if you *accept*, now, that life is not meant to be an easy path all the time. Accepting this means that you are *prepared* for the dark places, rather than being completely surprised and shattered when they come.

The important thing, of course, is that we will stand together in those difficult places ... which, as you realise, come just as easily to my younger as well as to My older followers. When those dark times come – often suddenly – think of My love straight away and see it all around your situation. Learn to recognise how much *more* painful life would be *without* Me.

Thank Me, frequently, that, because of My love, any time of darkness is only temporary, and that there are *always* better things ahead for you, as one who trusts Me.

Do not be afraid ... I will always help you.

(Isaiah 41.13)

95

There will be many temptations to follow other roads through your life. These temptations will be particularly strong when you are young. I have made it clear that the roads of fame, wealth, power and influence, though they may seem to satisfy a need in you, will lead precisely *nowhere* .

My child, when following *My* road, so much is given to you ... things which will give you a *deeper* joy. These will be the things which I see as right for the kind of person you are, and are becoming.

As the years go by, you will *know* how false are other roads, but, until then, I want you to believe My word that the only road worth following is that upon which you are now starting ... shared with Me.

**... all these things
will be given to you as well.**

(Matthew 6.33)

My child, think *often* about the future … as I do!

You cannot know exactly what lies ahead, but just be sure that your hand is in Mine. Be true to Me. Be true to loved ones and friends.

Show My love to others. Keep trusting, even when you find it hard to see the way.

You know that you will always be safe in My love.

I am *preparing* you for life in heaven …

Keep looking forward to this, because it is the one *certain* thing in My universe.

**In heaven,
a treasure is kept for you.**

(Luke 12.33)

My child, the name I had for my first disciples was *friends*...simply friend. A true friend is someone you can really trust, someone who will never let you down. Such a friend is a gift from me!

It is sad that an earthly friend can sometimes disappoint you. Remember that whenever you think that I have forgotten you, you will discover that all the time I have been thinking about you and preparing to help you.

My child, your situation is always near to my heart.

I have called you friends.

(John 15.15)

Because I made you, I know, perfectly the things that make up your character...the good things and the not so good.

This is why I warned about making judgments of others, simply because human knowledge is so imperfect.

If you judge in a kind way and see another person's good points, that is always pleasing to me.

I am sure that you see what is dangerous...critical attitudes usually based on lies infiltrating your mind.

Do not judge, or you, too, will be judged.
(Matthew 7.1)

The challenges lying ahead of you can often be frightening, and you may want to avoid them.

Always remember that I go ahead of you to make a challenge easier for you, or to remove it altogether!

If you pray about these things, I will *anticipate* life's difficulties on your behalf.

When you find that a thing turns out better than you feared, you can thank me that *I went before you!*

Be strong and courageous.

(Deuteronomy 31.7)

There are times when you are so upset that you can't even pray in the way you would like to. Even if you can't (for the moment), think what to say to Me, the one thing which can always do is to whisper to say my name – the name of Jesus.

When you speak my name, it tells me that I am in your thoughts, and it keeps out evil influences. You are then ready to think out what to say to me once more.

The name which is above every name.
(Phillipians 2.9)

Although heaven is hidden from normal sight it is not a place far distant or out-of-reach.

Whenever My love finds its way into a human heart that heart is in touch with heaven. Yes, even if you don't realise it!

For my love to find a way into the heart, give much time to thinking of that love – especially as you see it on the Cross.

In the Gospels, I invited all my children upon the earth "Come to Me". If you do this, you are showing me your wish to be part of heaven one day.

Christ in you.....the hope of glory.
(Colossians 1.21)

You have found that to show patience can sometimes be terribly hard. This is because the world so often tells you that you must have a thing quickly!

What you manage to achieve through hasty action seldom turns out successful.

Yes, my child, older people can learn a lesson from *you*, if you are calm and patient. You will be setting a good example.

You will need a little courage in refusing to be hasty, and I will help you.

May you have great endurance and patience.
(Colossians 1.11)

If you have a very good friend, someone you would be sorry to lose, that friend must be *valued*, so that you would not say or do things which would make you lose that friend.

Friendship is such an important matter to myself.

True friendship is something to value more than money, popularity, worldly status, and all the things which the world says are important.

A true friend sticks closer than a brother.
(Psalm 19.24)

Many human beings promise great rewards which are later found to be disappointing. This is why I commanded my children *not to covet*.

If the habit of covetousness is allowed to become part of person, that person is never satisfied with what he or she has.

A discontented person *never* finds true happiness.

Be content, whatever your circumstances.
(Phillipians 4.11)

My child, have you noticed how often people saying a word of thanks have a smile on their faces when doing so?

The smile is a sign of someone who is truly grateful, rather than the saying of thanks *without* a smile as just a formal recognition.

Cultivate the heart which is ready to respond with a sincere smile for even the smallest kindness.

The Lord loves a *cheerful* giver.
(2 Corinthians 9.7)

My child, you will have often felt ashamed after saying or doing what you know to have *been wrong*.

You know that I'm hurt by these things, which can happen so easily at times.

I will always draw near to listen to you when you are truly sorry, and then my love will sweep away the wrong things.

You must always trust my *mercy*. You must show that same mercy to others and not bear grudges.

I lift up those who are truly sorry.
(Isaiah 57.15)

My child, when you *really* want to be sure of my love, look again at the cross. Think about it often.

The Cross at Calvary is the place where the love I have *for my children is best seen,* as I have told you.

The Cross is where the world can see how far I am prepared to go to save the human race.

Remember always, My child, that the Cross was for *you....*

There is no greater love than when man lays down His life for His friends.

(John 15.13)

My child, never be afraid to be where there is silence!

I can be most clearly "heard" (whispers into the heart), when the noises of the world are shut out.

In quietness, that heart-peace which the world longs for is most able to reach you. It is above all a whisper of *love*....

How faint the whisper we hear of Him.
(Job 26.14)

That feeling of quiet satisfaction when you have been kind to someone is one of the things built into life.

Yes, even if the person you have been kind to is not immediately appreciative!

The feeling of satisfaction is really the sign of a good conscience...a conscience which will normally make you feel uneasy when you've said or done something wrong.

A conscience *kept in good order* will help you to negotiate the complexities of life safely.

My sheep listen to My voice.
(John 10.27)

Life can teach many lessons. Occasionally something causes a person to say "I *must* remember that; it is important" It is vital for your future to hold on to what I show you clearly at certain times.

If you fail to hold on to lessons learned, so much time is wasted in learning a lesson all over again.

Make it one of your life's rules to *act* upon what I show you vividly.

Anyone who hears my words and acts upon them is like a wise man who builds his house on the rock.
(Matthew 7.24)

The nature of life on the earth means that it is very easy to wander from a safe path.

I want you to realise that if you really trust Me as your Companion I will always make you aware where there is danger.

These are My *promptings*..... the quiet voice in the heart which you must learn to listen to and to trust.

My child I want you to avoid the often – painful consequences of wandering from the path of which I make you aware.

Enter through the narrow gate.
(Matthew 7.13)

It is not really important if you do not always *feel* courageous!

As long as you have Me in your life I give you courage to face occasions and challenges, even if you do not feel brave beforehand.

My child, My followers have always found that I have acted for them with strength which is not just their own.

You cannot *force* yourself to be brave, but you can, at any time, invite Me to act with you.

Your right hand upholds me.

(Psalm 6.38)

When I was on the earth I praised My friend Mary Magdalene for giving Me her time...time to listen to Me and to learn from Me.

My child, you must never be too busy to pray! Time spent with Me, in any place and at any time, is always time well spent.

My blessing is upon those times, so always look out for opportunities to talk with Me. I will show them to you.

...devote yourselves to prayer.
(1 Corinthians 7.5)

At the time of the Crucifixion, so many people behaved with hatred in their hearts – including those who claimed to be God-fearing.

Why did they suddenly behave in this way? The reason is that hidden forces of will entered their minds, causing them to choose the bad rather than the good.

On Good Friday, (as it became to be called) My human body was left of dead and those evil forces seemed to have won. But their victory was only for a short time, as you know. The resurrection on the third day was a victory for everyone.

Jesus said: "It is accomplished."
(John 19.30)

The forces of darkness opposed to Me always try to blind you to what is true.

You may be tempted to act against the way you see is right, saying to yourself "It doesn't matter, just for this occasion."

I constantly told My disciples that truth was very important because I knew that life on this earth works better when people live by the truth which is in their hearts.

I tell you the *truth*.

(John 6.53)

So many people are unhappy because they are always wishing that they had what others have got. Envy is a most serious state to be in and, although it may seem to quite harmless and almost neutral, it is sometimes called a "cardinal sin" (jealousy, when found in its most vicious forms).

Remember, My child, that in the events leading to My death on Calvary, envy, (growing into sheer hatred), was in so many hearts.

Because human beings do not know the truth in the way I do, envy can be completely misplaced.

Love not envy; it does not boast.
(1 Corinthians 13.4)

My child, the nature of life upon the earth is that you suddenly find yourself without a kind family member, or a trusted friend. Your life feels terribly empty, and you feel shattered inside. What can you do?

If you can manage to simply cling to the thought of Myself, I promise to give you a sense of My love for you to comfort you in your *loss*.

That sense of comfort will be there for you throughout your life whenever you need it.

I am the Lord who will always comfort you.
(Isaiah 66.13)

My child, have you already noticed that the most joyful people you know are those who are grateful for so many things in their lives?.....

Gratitude especially about the little things which the world takes for granted!

My child, let there be lots of "thank-you", as you notice what I have provided for you. A *grateful* heart, as I have told you so often, means a contented heart.

In everything, give thanks.
(1 Thessalonians 5.18)

Only I know – exactly – your past, present and future.

Whatever happens in your life is never a surprise to Me.

Because life is not always easy, the only really safe place to be is keeping as close as you possibly can to Me. Make up your mind to do this.

Underneath are God's everlasting arms.
(Deuteronomy 33.27)

My child, the only wealth worth setting your heart upon is *heavenly* treasure.

As you try to follow Me through your life, and if you want *only* Me as your reward, the treasure awaiting you will be a priceless one.

The treasure of heaven is to enjoy My love in the company of other souls who made Me their hope when they were on earth!

To be poor, yet having *real* wealth.
(Proverbs 13.7)

Before you settle down for the night, make sure that your last thoughts are of Me.

Do not let the jumble of impressions which have been that day trouble your spirit; turn away from all of them by looking to Me.

As you look into My countenance, let the thought of Me watching over you carry you over into the night hours, and make you truly peaceful.

I will lie down and sleep in peace.

(Psalm 4.8)

122

When you say a prayer for others, it goes beyond mere words. This is because I will be working in the heart of the person you prayed for – especially if you have asked that the person should come to know My love.

Very often, the person you said a prayer for will be unaware that you have been praying for them!

The prayer offered in faith can make a sick person well.
(James 5.15)

Never forget that human beings were made in My image. That is why I feel the pains and the joys of life, much as you do (except more strongly). Yes, My child, "in My image" means a divine friend who *understands*. Because of this, you must never be shy or hesitant about approaching Me.

I am gentle and humble in heart.

(Matthew 11.29)

My child, always resist the making of comparisons with others you know. Because your knowledge as a fellow human being is so limited, so partial, you dare not compare yourself with anyone. Especially, you must never see another person as lacking your own good points. This is spiritual pride. I see each one of My children with My own eye of truth. The lesson is always to look *only* at Me, and to be concerned about what I am doing.

Love is not proud.

(1 Corinthians 13.4)

Think of what it means to be My chosen child!

As I told My disciples, they did not choose Me, but I chose them. It was because I had already chosen *you*, that you reached out to find Me.

My choosing is something *permanent*. Even when there are many things which I wish to change in you, My choice of you will *remain* to affect the rest of your life. This is because of My faithfulness; and because I know what you will become.

Chosen from the beginning.

(2 Thessalonians 2.13)

The things which you have to decide are made so much easier if you look at them *in the light of My presence*. Be sure that you want to follow what I see is best.

When you learn to give every possibility to Me, you will find, more and more, that certain choices are made without you having even to think about them!

The Lord gives wisdom.
(Proverbs 2.6)

To walk in a way which is pleasing to Me is simply to think much about how I have cared for you.

Remember that, if that wish to please Me is there in you, you, are going to overcome many temptations.

If the wish to please Me is there, the strength you need is automatically *part of you*. My child, the using of My strength.....always.

Walk in God's light.
(1 John 1.7)

Even if a certain area of life always seems to defeat you I can take you into that sort of situation once more and make you victorious.

Trust Me to do so.

As you confront a difficulty once more, think of My light around you and thank me that, in My strength, you can do all things. You will soon begin to be victorious where once you were defeated.

I can do all things through Jesus Christ who strengthens me.
(Phillipians 4.13)

My child, there are so many careers and occupations you could follow which the world can use.

There is one ambition which will always please Me (even if people do not know, for the moment, that it is in your heart). That ambition is that you will be *used* to spread the Good News which I came to bring. I will always strengthen you in this.

May your kingdom come.
(Mattthew 6.10)

130

When you have given a problem to Me, it will help you not to feel the weight of the problem if you *thank* Me, every time whenever you think about the problem, that it is *in My hands*. This means that I am working for you, in what may be difficult for you, to bring about the best-possible solution. Yes, My child, My sure working.....

The ways of the Lord are sure.
(Psalm 19.9)

Because this life holds so many disappointments, you will often wonder if you were mistaken to be a follower of Mine.

It is a great sadness to Myself when one of My children tries to live without Me.

You will find that I use many circumstances to draw your heart back to Me. When you are trying to live without Me, you will often be restless until our relationship (always something precious to me) is restored.

Jesus said "Will you also go away?"
(John 6.67)

It often takes a whole lifetime before the lesson is learned of putting Me above everything else.

This always means wishing to find what I most desire for you....something which becomes almost automatic the more you practice it.

To ask yourself in difficult situations (in fact, in *every* situation), "what would Jesus, my Lord, want me to do here?"

That pause, (however brief), to sense *My* will for you, will mean a walk of increasing safety.

I will teach you in the way you should go.

(Psalm 32.8)

You are aware of times in your life when you feel completely alone. Even those who love you do not seem to understand or to sympathise.

I allow you to feel like this sometimes, so that you will appreciate Me as the One who does not change.

Loneliness is never really loneliness if you are aware that I am there with you....even if it is only a gentle presence.

....that we may live in His presence.

(Hosea 6.2)

When I was on the earth I said that to have Me in your life was like finding something so precious that you would sell everything else in order to make it your own.

My child, throughout your life, believe with all your heart that the one thing you could *not* buy (which you must always treasure), is *Myself*.

Peter said "Lord, You have the words of eternal life.
(John 6.68)

The reason why I will not let anything which happens on earth take you away from Me is that *My love for you just could not be stronger!*

The one ambition which the powers of evil have (even more than tempting you to wrong ways), is to separate you from Me.

You can guard against this by thinking of Me and talking to Me, *often*, through each day.

Nothing can separate us from God's love in Jesus our Lord.

(Romans 8.39)

Those who come to know Me are those of My children who *pursue* their growing knowledge.

Knowing Me is the greatest thing in the world and you can achieve this, no matter what others may tell you.

To pursue anything in life, means keeping a single aim and not letting anything tempt you away, or to make you give up.

Yes, My child, simply following Me closely... *No* turning back.

Jesus said "I am the Way".
(John 14.6)

There is often a time of waiting, as you have found before your most earnest prayers are answered. But the time is one which I always use. In that time of waiting trustingly, I develop your patience and your trust, ensuring the best possible answer. As you journey through life in My company the greater will be the quiet expectation that I *simply cannot* fail to provide an answer for you. As you can guess, the answer is already provided!

....through patience, to inherit what has been promised.

(Hebrews 6.12)

"**D**o I feel that this is what the Lord Jesus Himself *really* wants for me!" is a question needing to be asked. It is better not to go rushing into anything before asking oneself this question.

As I have told you, there is always an element of danger in self-will. This is avoided if you spend a few moments to seek that sense of My own wishes for you. What you are coming to realise is that when My wishes and your own are in agreement I am able more easily to grant the longings of your heart.

In quietness and trust is your strength.

(Isaiah 30.15)

Because I live in My children I made it very clear that when you are kind to someone, I receive as well!

In the same way, if you are able to help one of your brothers and sisters and neglect to do so, then I lose something which would have been a blessing for Myself. Therefore, always try to remember that I, your Lord, am touched by what you do.

In as much as you did it to the least of My brethren, you did it for Me.

(Matthew 25.40)

You will so often find that with a little more effort – just a little – victory in certain matters was very close for you.

If you are determined not to "give up", simply wait for a while and then try again, *using* My strength, and thanking Me for the victory which will come. My strength allied to your own, will turn so many times of "failure" into confidence – building successes, in things large and small.

Thanks be to God who gives us the victory through Jesus our Lord.
(1 Corinthians 15.57)

My child let Me be the *home of your thoughts*! In other words, always letting your thoughts come back to Me, whatever has been on your mind. Life's various desires can always unsettle you a little, if you do not let your thoughts return to Me again. With practice, it will become almost automatic to make *Me* the home of your thoughts.

Let your minds be filled with everything that is true...
(Philippians 4.8)

My child, if you try to keep Me in your thoughts through your life, you will find that all the promises which I have given will come true.

At the end of your life, there is a promise for you which will come true, along with all the others...that I will take you to be in My heavenly Kingdom.

No one else can give you that hope for your future. Just make sure that you return to Me even if you wander into wrong ways, for only a little while.

The things which are unseen last forever.
(2 Corinthians 4.18)

My child, all that really matters is what you will become.

You will not know exactly what the future holds, but be sure that your hand is in Mine.

Be true to Me. Be true to loved ones and friends. Keep trusting, even when the way grows dark, you will always be completely safe in My love, if you go on trusting. I am *preparing* you for the life in My kingdom which I have promised.

My child, I want you to look forward to this...as I do. Heaven is the one certain thing in My creation.

Take heart! I have overcome the world.
(John 16.33)

Both Original Standard and Young People's editions
of I Am With You *are available from the Publisher:*

John Hunt Publishing Ltd., Laurel House,
Station Approach,
Alresford, Hants, SO24 9JH, UK

or from:

Good News Books
Upper Level, St John The Apostle Church Complex
296 Sundon Park Road
Luton, Beds, LU3 3AL
E-mail: orders@goodnewsbooks.net
http://www.goodnewsbooks.net
Tel: 01582 571011

Bridge Books and Music
14 North Bridge Street, Sunderland
Tyne and Wear, SR5 IAB, England

Also available by John Woolley:

Meet Jesus (for children)

Available from New Life and Bridge Books:

Getting to Know Jesus *(for 11-14 year olds)*
Hello Jesus *(for 7-1 0 year olds)*

THE "I AM WITH YOU" FELLOWSHIP

Readers of Fr John's inspired words may join the
I Am With You Fellowship. All in the Fellowship
are remembered in prayer and are encouraged to
write about any particular need. To join, please send
your name, address (incl. postcode), phone number
and email address (if available) to:-

I Am With You Foundation
c/o Goodnews Books, Upper Level,
St John the Apostle Church Complex,
296 Sundon Park Road,
Luton, Luton, Beds, LU3 3AL
01582 571011
email: orders@goodnewsbooks.net
www.goodnewsbooks.net

The Fellowship distributes mini copies of
John Woolleys books free of charge all over the world.
If you would like to make a donation in support of this
work please send it to:-

I Am With You Foundation
2 Lauradale Road
London N2 9LU, UK
Tel 0208 883 2665
Email:- contact@iamwithyou.co.uk

For further information, please visit our website:-
www.iamwithyou.co.uk